Children's Authors

J. K. Rowling

Cari Meister
ABDO Publishing Company

visit us at
www.abdopub.com

Published by ABDO Publishing Company, 4940 Viking Drive, Suite 622, Edina, Minnesota
55435. Copyright © 2001 Abdo Consulting Group, Inc., Pentagon Tower, P.O. Box 36036,
Minneapolis, Minnesota 55435 USA. International copyrights reserved in all countries. No part
of this book may be reproduced in any form without written permission from the publisher.

Published 2001
Printed in the United States of America
Second Printing 2002

Photos: AP/Wideworld, Corbis
Editors: Bob Italia, Kate A. Furlong, Tamara L. Britton, Christine Fournier
Art Direction: Pat Laurel, Neil Klinepier

Library of Congress Cataloging-in-Publication Data

Meister, Cari.
    J.K. Rowling / Cari Meister.
        p. cm. -- (Children's authors. Set 2)
    Includes bibliographical references and index.
    ISBN 1-57765-482-X
     1. Rowling, J. K.--Juvenile literature. 2. Authors, English--20th
century--Biography--Juvenile literature. 3. Women and
literature--England--History--20th century--Juvenile literature. 4. Potter, Harry
(Fictitious character)--Juvenile literature. 5. Children's stories--Authorship--Juvenile
literature. [1. Rowling, J. K. 2. Authors, English. 3. Women--Biography.] I. Title. II.
Series.

PR6068.O93 Z77 2001
823'.914--dc21
[B]
                                                                          00-052208

Contents

J. K. Rowling

J. K. Rowling is the author of the popular Harry Potter books. Her stories have become the favorites of children across the globe.

J. K., known as Joanne to her friends, was born in a small town in England. She grew up in a family that loved to read. Joanne wrote her first story by the time she was six. During her years as a student, Joanne continued to read and write stories.

After college, Joanne took a job as a secretary. But she was bad at the job. And she disliked it. So she moved to Portugal and worked as a teacher. She spent her free time writing about a wizard named Harry Potter.

Joanne stayed in Portugal for a few years. Then she moved to Scotland. There, she finished working on the Harry Potter book. Then her agent helped her get it published.

Joanne's book quickly became a hit in England. Soon it was published in other countries. Children and adults could not get enough of their new favorite character, Harry Potter.

J. K. Rowling

Young Joanne

*J*oanne Kathleen Rowling was born in Chipping Sodbury, England, on July 31, 1965. Her parents were Peter and Ann Rowling. Peter managed an aircraft factory. Ann worked as a lab **technician**. Joanne also had a younger sister named Di.

The Rowlings often read to Joanne when she was young. When she grew older, Joanne liked to read in her free time. Her favorite books were *The Little White Horse* by Elizabeth Goudge and *Manxmouse* by Paul Gallico. She also liked the Narnia books by C. S. Lewis.

Joanne enjoyed making up her own stories. She wrote her first story when she was six. It was about a rabbit named Rabbit. In the story, Rabbit had the **measles**. Many friends came to visit him, including a giant bee called Miss Bee. Joanne knew even then that she wanted to be a writer.

When Joanne was young, her family moved twice. First they moved to a town called Yate. A short time later, they moved to a nearby town called Winterbourne.

In Winterbourne, Joanne made friends with many neighborhood children. She especially liked playing with her good friends Ian and Vikki Potter.

Winterbourne, England

School Days

When Joanne was nine, her family moved to a town called Tutshill. It was near the River Wye. Joanne and her friends liked to play by the river.

Joanne attended Tutshill Primary School. On Joanne's first day, the teacher gave a test on fractions. Joanne had never learned fractions. She failed the test. So the teacher put Joanne in the "stupid" row.

Joanne was **embarrassed**. Everyone at her new school thought she was dumb. But Joanne worked hard. And at the end of the year, Joanne was allowed to sit in the "smart" row.

While at Tutshill, Joanne continued to write stories. She also read often. One of her favorite authors was Jane Austen. Joanne admired the details in Austen's writing. She used them as a model for her own stories.

After Tutshill, Joanne attended Wyedean Comprehensive School. Joanne felt like an outsider at Wyedean. She was very quiet. And she preferred reading instead of playing sports.

Slowly, things at Wyedean improved for Joanne. She found a group of friends with similar interests. They loved listening to Joanne's wonderful stories.

By her last year at Wyedean, Joanne had become more **confident**. She was outgoing in her classes. Her grades were high. And she was named Head Girl. This meant she gave tours to people who visited Wyedean. And she gave a speech at graduation.

Jane Austen

Hello, Harry!

After Wyedean, Joanne attended the University of Exeter in Devon, England. She studied **literature** and French. As a student, she lived in Paris, France, for a year.

After graduating from Exeter, Joanne worked as a secretary. But she was not good at it. Joanne was very disorganized. And sometimes she wrote stories instead of doing her work. This angered her bosses.

Joanne usually took the train to work. One day in 1990, the train she was riding broke down. As she waited, Joanne stared out the window at some cows.

Suddenly, she had an idea for a new story. She would write about a young wizard. His name would be Harry Potter, after her childhood friends in Winterbourne.

Joanne grew excited about Harry Potter. She knew it was a great story. She spent all her free time working on it.

But then Joanne's life changed suddenly. Her mom died unexpectedly. And she was unhappy with her job. Joanne needed to get away. So in 1991, she moved to Oporto, Portugal.

In Portugal, Joanne worked as an English teacher. She taught in the afternoons and evenings. She spent her mornings writing about Harry Potter.

While in Portugal, Joanne met Jorge Arantes. He was a Portuguese journalist. The two quickly fell in love and got married. Joanne continued to work on the Harry Potter book. She rewrote the first chapter ten times!

Oporto, Portugal

Hard Times

*I*n 1993, Joanne had a daughter named Jessica. Shortly after Jessica's birth, Joanne got divorced. This made her sad. She missed her family. And she had to take care of her baby all by herself. Joanne did not know what to do.

One day, her sister Di called. Di lived in Edinburgh, Scotland. She suggested that Joanne move to Edinburgh. Joanne thought a change would be good. So she and Jessica moved to Scotland in 1993.

At first, life was difficult. Joanne wanted to get a job. But she could not afford child care. So Joanne had to stay home and watch Jessica. Joanne received **welfare**. And she borrowed money from friends. Many people looked down on her because she was a poor, single mother.

Despite all of this, Joanne still had hopes for her Harry Potter book. She decided to finish the book and try to get it published.

Joanne disliked writing in her small, cold apartment. So she walked to Nicholson's Café. There, she wrote about Harry

Potter while Jessica napped beside her. In 1995, Joanne finished writing *Harry Potter and the Philosopher's Stone*.

Joanne knew she needed an **agent** if she wanted her book published. So she typed copies of the book. She sent the copies to two agents and waited for their response.

While Joanne waited, she began working as a French teacher. Soon, she did not need **welfare** any longer. Joanne's hard times were finally over.

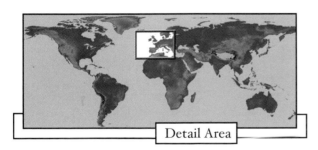

Detail Area

Western Europe

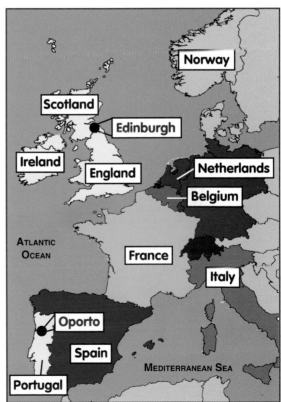

Norway

Scotland

Edinburgh

Ireland

England

Netherlands

Belgium

ATLANTIC OCEAN

France

Italy

Oporto

Spain

MEDITERRANEAN SEA

Portugal

Getting Published

*O*ne day, Joanne received a letter in the mail. It was from an **agent** named Christopher Little. He wanted to help Joanne get her Harry Potter book published. He warned her she would not make much money. But Joanne did not care. She just wanted to see her book in bookstores.

Little sent Joanne's book to several publishers. They all **rejected** it. But in 1996, Bloomsbury Publishing agreed to publish the book. Joanne was excited. Her dream had finally come true. Soon after, Joanne won a **grant** from the Scottish Arts Council. It gave her money to keep writing.

In 1997, Bloomsbury published *Harry Potter and the Philosopher's Stone*. English children loved the story. They began telling their friends about it. Before long, adults were reading it, too. Joanne's book had become a great success.

Opposite page: J. K. Rowling's popularity began in England and spread to the U.S. one year later.

Joanne continued to write about Harry Potter. Bloomsbury published her second book in 1998. It was called *Harry Potter and the Chamber of Secrets*. Just like the first book, the second one was a huge success in England.

An American **editor** named Arthur Levine noticed Joanne's books. Levine worked for a book publisher called Scholastic, Inc. He thought young Americans would love Harry Potter, too. So Levine bought the **rights** to sell Joanne's book in the U.S.

Scholastic paid Joanne more money than any other first-time children's author. The money let Joanne stop working as a teacher and begin writing full time. It also allowed her to afford a nice house and a computer.

In 1998, Scholastic published Joanne's first book in America. Scholastic changed the title to *Harry Potter and the Sorcerer's Stone*. The book quickly caught on with American children and adults. Soon, the American movie company Warner Brothers even began planning a Harry Potter movie!

American readers have purchased more than 800,000 copies of **Harry Potter** *and the* **Sorcerer's Stone.**

Wild About Harry

When Joanne was not busy writing, she spent time on book tours. She traveled through Europe and America. She talked to young Harry Potter fans and signed their books. She also gave **interviews** to newspapers and magazines.

Scholastic published two more of Joanne's books in 1999. In the summer, *Harry Potter and the Chamber of Secrets* came out. That fall, *Harry Potter and the Prisoner of Azkaban* was released. Both books quickly became best-sellers.

In 2000, Scholastic published Joanne's fourth book. It was called *Harry Potter and the Goblet of Fire*. Children stood in lines at bookstores for hours waiting for their own copies. Many stores ran out of books in just a few minutes.

Joanne's books are not just popular in the U.S. and England. Joanne's books are sold in more than 100 countries. And they are printed in more than 40 languages. Joanne's first four books have sold more than 76 million copies worldwide.

*Children in Shanghai, China, got their first look at Harry Potter books in 2000. This boy is looking at the Chinese edition of **Harry Potter and the Sorcerer's Stone**.*

The Harry Potter books have earned Joanne many awards. She won the **Nestlé Smarties Gold Award** in 1997, 1998, and 1999. She won the 1999 **Whitbread Children's Book of the Year** award for *Harry Potter and the Prisoner of Azkaban*. And her first three books were named **ALA Notable Children's Books** in 1999 and 2000.

Joanne's books have brought her worldwide fame. But that has not changed how she writes. She still likes to write in **longhand** while sipping coffee at a café. She is a very **disciplined** writer. She writes every day. Sometimes she writes 11 hours a day.

Joanne plans to write a total of seven Harry Potter books. She will write one book for each year that Harry is in school. After she finishes the Harry Potter series, Joanne is unsure what she will do next. But one thing is certain. Joanne will continue to write, which is what she loves best.

Opposite page: J. K. Rowling poses on a book tour while promoting **Harry Potter and the Goblet of Fire.**

Glossary

agent - a person who represents another person in business matters.

ALA Notable Children's Book - an annual award given out by the American Library Association. Books are chosen for quality, style, and excellence.

confident - sure of one's self.

disciplined - showing self-control.

editor - a person who makes sure a piece of writing has no errors in it before it is published.

embarrass - to feel ashamed or uncomfortable.

grant - a gift of money that is to be used for a special purpose.

interview - a meeting where one person or group gives another information.

literature - writing that has lasting value because of its excellence.

longhand - ordinary writing by hand in which all the words are written out in full.

measles - an illness that causes a fever and rash.

Nestlé Smarties Gold Award - an award given by Nestlé to an author living in the United Kingdom. Children pick the winner.

reject - to refuse to take something.

rights - a legal claim to something.

technician - a person who is skilled at a specific task.

welfare - money that the government gives people in need.

Whitbread Children's Book of the Year - an award sponsored by the Whitbread Breweries. It is given out to books that are well written and popular among a wide range of readers.

Internet Sites

The Official Harry Potter Internet Site
http://www.scholastic.com
Click on the "Harry Potter" section to find out what's new, learn more about J. K. Rowling, or test your wizard trivia.

Write to J. K. Rowling at:
Scholastic, Inc.
555 Broadway
New York, NY 10012-3999

Index